From
My Healing
Heart

Maria Danahe Rodriguez Muro

Fulton Books
Meadville, PA

Published by Fulton Books 2024

ISBN 979-8-89221-075-1 (paperback)
ISBN 979-8-89221-076-8 (digital)

Printed in the United States of America

To my family

Acknowledgments

My Parents

Thank you for being the wind beneath my wings.
For never giving up on me and for understanding
me even when I couldn't understand
myself. For accepting me as I was, for who I
became, and for who I'm yet to become.

My Children
Isabel, Marlene, Nathan, and Liam

There is no better gift than the one I was
granted when I was given the honor to be
your mom. You have been the reason why I
keep pushing forward. You have kept me alive
through the most turbulent moments of my
life, even without your knowing. You gave
me the strength and will to want to continue
fighting to become a better version of myself.
Thank you for being the amazing, loving children
that you are, for being my support and my friends,
and for being the pillars that have kept my broken
and healing heart safe with your love and nurture.
Eternally grateful, eternally blessed
Psalm 23:1–6

Ascend

Connect to the oneness, embracing yourself whole,
expanding in awareness, and letting everything
flow.

Flow as the currents of the river.
Connecting with everything you touch.

Be willing and open to embody the greatness within you.
Expanding in awareness and embracing yourself whole.

Breathe

Breathe!
Ground yourself, to the things that soothe you.
Honor yourself in the sounds that heal you.
Feel how your lungs expand to the rhythm of your
    breathing.
Dancing in symphony to the beating of your heart.

Breathe!

It's difficult to understand and process the phases one must endure through the healing journey after a broken heart. Whether it is due to grieving death, divorce, childhood trauma, abuse, or mental health, we are never prepared to endure the pain and the aftermath.

The part where you have nothing but yourself is made to find the strength within to survive. It's in that space that you come face-to-face with finding who you truly are.

I wrote this, *From My Healing Heart*, in the hopes that it reaches your heart and helps you know that you are on the right path. Even in those moments in which you feel you can't go on and all is collapsing, don't give up.

It does get better; you will be okay.

Maria

Through my healing journey, I've encountered marvelous people who have helped me heal and reach the deeper ends of my heart and soul as I accompany them on their own healing journey.

"By the Sea" was written after a guided meditation session with a very dear friend. Our hearts can hold so many treasures, just as they can hold so much pain and shame.

Healing is transforming, and it allows you to know that it's okay to feel hurt and misunderstood. It's okay to be vulnerable, and once you are ready, it's okay to forgive and let go.

By the Sea

Without seeing, without knowing,
with open arms, I met you by the sea!
By the shore touching your toes,
it's calming waves hit your toes
to ease away the anxiety of your soul.

In that moment, I held your fragile soul,
close to my heart, and with a promise.
To always be there for you,
and hold you like my nurtured child.
Until the end of time!

As you heal, I'll heal.
As you shine, I'll shine.
As you smile, I'll smile.
As you rise, I rise.

I will hold your hand until the day you bloom.
Until the day you see the love within.
And the light you are, and not only what you are.
But what you can give.
I am here.

Chin Up

Stand up tall!
I know it hurts.
I know it's hard.

Look up!
Don't miss out on what is around you.
You light up the dark in your own path.
There's more to life; you'll find it!
When you look up and move from what's behind you.

Chin up.
You will be fine.

Cleanse My Soul!

Wash it all away.
What I was once,
that no longer serves me.

Take it all away!
Who once was,
that no longer knows me.
The false thoughts
that don't support me,
Wash it all away.

Bring me to awareness
to love
to peace
to strength
to beauty
Bring me to my higher self!

Embrace Yourself with Love!

Yes, all feels as if it's crumbling.
It feels as if a tornado came through
Taking down everything it could
Ripping things out, right from its root
It's confusing and painful.

The heart feels empty, why?
Know that it's part of the process to reconstruct
And become a better version of you.
What feels as empty and painful, it's the fear of the
  unknown.
You step out of your comfort zone and now you stand
Where you have no control of what is to come.
When your heart and soul begin to heal, it feels like
  a void.
But it's really that space that cleared out of the burden
  you carried for so long.
As you release, transformation begins to take place.
You begin to grow into the person you are meant to be.
Into the person who's been screaming loud to be let
  out from within.

It's the marvelous and powerful strength you kept,
  thinking you didn't have.
Now it's time to let go and take off; you embark your
  journey to self-love.
Breathe, it's time for you to rise and bloom.

Evaporated

Vanished into thin air
I can still feel you.
It's strange... You're still here
Only now you're fading.

Perhaps...
I held on to your essence,
To the character I built.
The character created by my
Heart and mind of who I thought
You could be.

It vanished...
It's gone.
The idea, the dream, the perception!
The version I made of you
It's drifting away.
The last fragrance
The last thought.

I'm free... Now that you're gone.

Hear Me

Grant me the strength.
To let go of what isn't for me.
Help me be grounded and allow the healing energy.
To flow and detach from my deepest
roots what hurts and holds me back.

Allow what is meant for me to touch my soul.
With ease, peace, and calmness.

Bring me the ability to recognize what is meant.
To flow back to me and let go of
what isn't meant to stay.
Grant me the strength to give love and be
patient, stay kind and be understanding.

Give me the courage to rise.
To my power and wisdom.
And to claim what is mine.
So it is...

I'm Here

Hear me
When you are in despair
When your soul feels empty

Hear me
When you feel lost and can't go on

Hear me
When your heart is hurt
When your mind is blocked

Hear me
When life feels heavy
When you don't know where to go

For here I am
Holding you tight
Lighting your path
Healing your heart
Leading your soul

Hear me

Joanna

Rooms of wisdom locked inside your heart
Rooms that no one has been into, your sacred soul.
Walking in loving grace
Through the pink roses held
within you; in your masked
Elegance, covered by your fearless strength!
Moving through your sacred place.

Ohh! If only you could see how
full of wonder your heart is!
I see it... I feel it... Why don't you?
Perhaps, in due time, you will
As you heal, the world will see
The light that's eager to be seen
You're rising, and I'm here to see
Joanna, believe!

Listen

Listen to the
silence, to the wind
To the scented memories
Your heart brings

Memories of the past
A past that helped build
Who you came to be

Have no fear!
Your path is clear
Do you hear the call?
A new journey is calling

Listen!
Listen closely!
Your time is here!

Seen

I close my eyes… I see you.
I call upon you… I feel you.
You're far, yet you're here.
Crazy, isn't it?
To feel your touch without having it.
To listen to your call without hearing it!
To hold you close to me and feel your heart through
    your eyes that stay still on your picture.

I see you.

Slow down
Shelter your heart and mind
From the perception of others

Rise up and embody
The love and strength within you
You are what you need

Take Me

Take me...to the place within my soul
Where I can unwind and be myself
Take me...to the deepest end of my chambers
Help me find the answers I seek.
Take me... Show me the many
magical colors that make me
Show me the amazing melody and
flow found within the dancing
Purples blending into the pinks
and greens of my soul.
Take me...where the light touches my path
Highlighting the scars that brought
me to rise to my higher self.
Understanding the pain that
caused them was minimal
Compared to the magical effect they would have as
I walked past what caused it.
Enhancing all that I've encountered,
changing me as it touched me.
Take me...to the place of freedom and peace
That leads my thoughts into words
that are meant to be read and felt
Take me.

To Be Seen

How ironic, isn't it?
To want to be seen by
The one you love.
To want to be felt and
Touched in ways you've never felt before…
No… it's not the physical touch or
That physical way of seeing…
It's beyond that!
To be seen through
Your heart and core.
To be seen through your skin into your soul.

Ironic, isn't it?
Being invisible, being present.
To hear spoken words without listening.
Ironic, isn't it?
To reminisce and listen.
To look back and see.
To want that touch
Through your skin and soul.
To want to be seen through your heart and core.

To seek for my soul, now that is gone.

Transform

Let your wings be free!
Let them expand and fly!
Release everything that no longer serves you.
MOVE FORWARD
Raise your vision, see how big the path is ahead!
You're not stuck.
You're growing.
YOU'RE RISING

Unique
Powerful You

The love you give,
Is not equal to the love you get.
You love with your heart.
Others love with theirs.

You give your all.
You give what you make of yourself.
So does everyone else...
For that reason, we don't always get the same we give.
You Know what you give is real and rare.
While others might still be trapped looking outside.
For what's hidden within themselves.

Warrior

You prepared me
To be loving, kind, and strong

Life tested my faith
You stood beside me

At my lowest
You showed me mercy and gave me love

You show me the way to you
Through the new paths you
open for me to walk into

A warrior! You say I am
My battle?
That's against my own self

Be courageous... You tell me
I am with you... You remind me
It will be okay... You assure me

I am your child; I am you warrior

Why do we run?
Do we even know we are running?

Stop running
Show up…for you
Commit…to you
Fight…for you

Don't let go…of you and your dreams
Don't give up… Even when all seems to fail

Learn to live life for you, because at
the end you create for you
Stay still… Stop running

To Be Seen!
Part 2

Ironic, isn't it?
To yearn for love, to see you.
To wish to be touched and feel it as you've never felt
   before.
No! It's not the physical touch or the physical way
   of seeing!
It's beyond that!

Ironic, isn't it?
To question the ways of the universe.
To see your wishes granted but wonder why in the
   way they are given!
Real, yet distant.
Intense, yet so far.
Through my eyes, you see me.
Invisible, you hold me!
You reach deep through my heart and soul.
Touching me in ways I've never been touched before.
I feel you, and you're not present.
I listen without hearing…

Ironic, isn't it?
I'm invisible, but present.
I feel you through my heart and core.
You see me through my skin, deep into my soul.

I find you in the moving waves of your spirit.
You hold me close to you and meet me eye to eye.
In your soul, I lose myself.
Not in the words you tell me.
But in the welcoming sound played by your hazel
    eyes.
As I find my way into your heart and soul.

Ironic, isn't it?
In the distance…you see me! Without touching me, I
    feel you… In your soul, I'm seen.

Left to Die... To Rise

Into the open ocean, you dropped me.
You knew I would drown.
Left to die in the darkness.
I'm afraid of the monsters in the dark.

Fading away in the depths of eternal sleep,
A warm hand touched me.
To awaken her child, the moon held me.
And showed me that, just like her, I have light!

Hear me, sweet child,
It's only dark at night!
The king's son will protect you.
When I turn my sides, as I must vanish.
For a new moon to rise.
You are darkness, light, water, earth, and fire!
Yet you're afraid to survive?

RISE, MOON CHILD!
Stand tall to your light.
Drown into the depths of your soul.
That's where you've been all along!
Don't you know?
In the darkness, you rise!

For a new moon to come, a new cycle must start!
Total darkness is there for a new you to rise!
Now SEE WITH YOU!
Now listen with your heart!
In your darkness,
A GODDESS now stands!
Shining in the skin made of stardust,
In an armor coming from the sun,
Through your eyes, the brightness of the moon
    shines!

Released into the open ocean to die, you thought!
But in the darkness of your naked soul,
An armored goddess ascended and, in loving power
    and tender ruling,
A high priestess was born.

For there to become a goddess, in your wounded soul
    you stood.
Rising in wisdom and growth.

My Idea of Love

My idea of love
Was thinking in the feeling
Coming from the protective embrace of the love that
would come to save me
Caressing me, kissing me…telling me I was his all

In a turn of events, life taught me;
I am my savior
I am that love
I am my protector
Love is real
I am love
Love is you!

Higher Self

Unknown
Untamed
Release yourself from the version of you
That in the past served you.
Today you are no longer that person.
Today you embrace the new you.

It scares you! I know!
Your higher self speaks.
I'm here for you.
Let me take you.
Let me guide you.
Let me show you the greatness of your soul!

Trust me, let her go!
Hold me; I won't let go!
Don't resist me; it's time to go!

When the Sun Speaks

Lost in your powerful and magnetic look,
Bright energy vibrating on your sides.
The king sun speaks through his
spinning rings of light!
Words of wisdom, love, and peace.
Through my eyes, I see him.
Through my soul, I feel him.
As he heals my ascending soul.
Dressing me in golden dust,
Dropping his armor on my sleeves.
Embedded in blooming roses,
Shining and strong!
As his rays of power flow,
A dress is given to cover my scarring soul.
A warrior, glowing in glory and love.

Rising goddess, rising soul,
Embrace your body in this dress of love!
Divine feminine, divine beauty, divine you!

In my golden power, you now stand.
Keep rising! Keep glowing! Keep reaching!
Keep searching, my sweet divine child!

The sun king has chosen.
The sun king has spoken.

You are divine; you are his child!

Death...My Teacher

How do you think you'll die?
I think I already died, many times.
I don't think of dying; death does not scare me.
I've felt pain while dying, while living.
Horrifying pain to let go a part
of me, to be born again.
Into a better version of myself.

Death has come to me.
Not to shut my eyes in eternal sleep,
But to make me feel the pain of
being alive without living!

I am strange, weird...kooky.
Because I chose to be me.
Death has been a remote thought in my mind.
I didn't understand that death could be so painful.
I feared leaving my body, I thought.
I'd rather sleep forever than feel again,
but that thought is no longer there.

Like a tortured soul, inflicting many wounds
by trying to fit into the expectations, needs,
Perceptions of others. Lost within the box
of convenience, death came to me.
Eye to eye, I faced her without any fears.

I decided, I would learn to be alive, in
my own skin and my own soul.
In my own authentic ways, dying every
night to be reborn every morning.

Death is not to be feared.
Death is a state of mind.
Death is a teacher.

When my body falls into eternal sleep,
I will know that my turn in this physical
plane has come to an end.
But even then, it's not the end of me.
For now, I am alive—living, loving, being.
Death is always with me.
Happiness is all around.
In the flow of the water,
In the stillness of the rocks,
In the changing colors of the sky,
In the gentle whispers among the wind and trees.
Everything fulfilling a purpose,
To nurture your heart and soul.

Happiness is you!

Somewhere beneath the Chaos

Beneath my aching heart
I found the pieces of myself
I had neglected to see
Somewhere in the chaos
Within my rising soul
I found a shield and an armor
Given for my silent battles
Against the giants I fought alone.

Somewhere in my journey
In front of a mirror, I stood
Reflecting before me, a goddess spoke
It's time to rise further
It's time to shine brighter
It's time for your voice to be heard
It's time for your voice to be loud.

Somewhere in the chaos of my healing soul
Beneath it all, I found what I always wanted
Freedom and love.

Sweet Child

In the depths of your soul...there is your love.
Within the treasures in your heart...there is your
　　wisdom.
Rooted in your heart...there is your strength.
Why should you doubt who you are?

Sweet Child

Beauty flows in your acts of kindness.
In your eyes, the gifts of your soul are hidden.
Like two open windows, they reveal the treasures of
　　your heart!
Sing to the notes of your words of wisdom!
Dance to the healing colors of your divine spirit.
Feel the strength gained through your healed wounds.
Don't doubt, my sweet child.

Sweet Child

Gleam across the paths you touch.
See how far your brightness goes!
No doubt, my child.
I know who you are!

Do you?

Grow confident!
And in love with who you are.
Remember:
The ego is impatient.
Because it's limited.
Your spirit is patient.
Because it knows it's eternal!

Flow as the currents of the river
Connecting with everything you
touch...
Willingly be open to embody
The greatness within you
Expanding in awareness
And embracing yourself whole

Let your emotions
Flow at the pace of the current
Let your heart open
To the touch of what heals you
See...listen...feel with your heart
Everything will be okay

Where you can flow
At your own rhythm, in comfort,
at peace
That's where you belong

Feel your soul as it nourishes
Hear your heart as it heals
Open your heart to the gifts of your spirit
You ARE RISING

The embrace of a new beginning
Starts in knowing you have changed
This is a new you
Stronger, wiser, unbreakable!
There is courage in embracing change!

I Live!

Within the patterns of my healing soul
I find fears…insecurities, and emotions
Tied to the loss of trust and abandonment
Hidden beneath the false idea
that I'm unworthy of love
I find the still fresh wounds I've
been neglecting to turn to.

I come forward from a humbling space of love
And self-reflection
To forgive who I was
And embrace who I'm becoming.

I vow to myself to remain true to myself.
I am worthy!
I welcome love.
I forgive myself and forgive others.
I let go of the past.
Of who I was.
And who is not meant to stay.

I live.

Untold Stories

Trapped in my chest
Sometimes for days, weeks...years
Untold stories...
Of an aching heart, lost in its grief
A grief unique to the universe I am.

Untold stories...
Of the path I traveled just to become
Not knowing I was supposed to get lost
To reconnect with myself and go
in the quest to find me.

Untold stories...
Of happiness masking the distress
and despair held within
Held so tight by that girl I once was.

Untold stories...
Of the hardened surface of my soul
Learning to be soft again
Learning to disarm the urge to keep my armor up
So no weapon could enter into my heart once more.

Untold stories...
Of the courage masking the fear beneath my skin
Of the woman I'm becoming,
fighting with the woman I was
And the woman I am today...opening to change.

Untold stories
Many untold stories
Some written in his journal of life
Some locked into the chest in my heart
And some washed away by the sea
Untold stories of me.

Untold stories engraved in the air.
Made famous by the moving waves.
Stories of me.
Unexpectedly, life changes.
Unexpectedly, love comes.
Without knowing, you are different.
Without knowing, fear sneaks through...
That's just because everything is new.
Let your heart be open!
For what is meant for you!

What Is Freedom?

We search for freedom
Tied up in the chains
Of limiting beliefs
Bounded by the fears
Of stepping into the unknown...

Curled up in the darkness,
We long for the idea of something different.
Holding on to what is expected from us to be!
Drowning within the tears of our soul,
Our spirit speaks—softly and
tender—yet it's hard to hear!
Don't be afraid; it tells you.
You light the path; you are more than this.
You are not tied into an unbreakable chain.
You have the power to break free.

It takes time; it takes courage
But then, it happens...you can see
You find the strength hidden beneath the fear
The courage you held inside that
you didn't know you had
You find the light within your soul
You stand tall, chin up, and embrace
who you have been all along.

With no fear of the unknown
You break the chains
Those that had been pulling you back
You take the blind off
That blocked you from seeing further out
Than what you thought you could see.

Freedom, what is freedom?
Learning to see with your soul!
Moving forward to the rhythm of your beating heart
Rising higher, discovering, and creating
without the holdbacks of the past
Freedom is you and your own feelings
to the wild wind moving your soul
Away from the darkness, delivering
you to the empowering journey
Of who you are yet to become!

It Speaks, You Know? The Ocean!

Vibrating words of wisdom,
Calming sounds of love!
Easing down the anger, the hurt.

Pulling you in and out,
Reminding your heart to beat.
Reminding you to live!
Taking with him,
The sorrows only he can feel.

The Quest

It was a quest…
A quest I didn't know I had.

One I needed to embark where
I needed to feel rejected.
A quest where I needed to get lost.
To find myself.

It was in this quest that I realized,
The value I give myself,
Is the most important.
I am important.

Here, in this quest, I learned,
What is meant for me, will be!

Like the Sunflower...

Grow strong in who you are
So you know yourself enough
To know what makes you strong and valuable
That even if the light is behind you
Thinking you're oblivious to its existence
You know that no matter your position
You're fully aware of the time
When its brightness makes you stronger.

Trust…It Vanished

I trusted easily, once
With my heart
My wounds
My deepest scars
It's hard to open my heart to someone—to anyone

It's hard to be reminded
That not all that shows you kindness is love
Most are driven by how you make people feel
Until you run out of strength to keep giving

Trust you? you ask
That vanished
Mid-second from when you forgot
Your knife has two sides
And without care
You cut me with it
Deep into my heart
Deep into my soul

The Ghost You Are

When you dropped me from up high,
You went on with your life.
Adventuring to new places with a new arm by your
  side,
You fulfilled my bucket list.
As if you had built it, to bring her up high,
Not knowing you thought of me when you handed
  her that pass.
While all this is happening,
I lost sight of who I was.
And picked up my pieces,
Putting them aside.

I walked away with a treasure no one can ever find.
I held on tight to our children and hugged them
  really tight!
In your absence, they are growing, living a life, not
  missing a moment of your adventures outside.
I befriended death, through the ghost you are.
She taught me rebirths are greater than my past, and
  that bucket list wasn't for you and me.
I put myself back together with a new sight.
Learned more after dying and losing sight of who I was.
Remembering I will always shine.
In my growth, I've felt pain.
But I never give up.

I met with the ocean, and he taught me to bargain,
Your skin for my peace, and the contract I signed,
For the high tide to take you away and far.

You thought you killed me on that last encounter in
our gray car.
When you said I was worthless, but I knew I would
rise.
See…you brought me to life, making me a mother
four times!

I see your reflection was tagged in my soul.
But the moon lit up my vision, while sitting in the
dark.
Afraid, I removed it, leaving a small mark; the
reminder I need not to ever turn back.

Today I forgive you.
I continue to rise; as the empress, I release you,
To continue in your circular path.
Until the day comes for you to look up and find the
treasure you left, blinded by your sinful eyes,
Guarded by the queen of swords as she keeps rising
until the end of time.

Let it flow
Let it go
Release it all
What hurts your heart
What troubles your mind
Forgive…
Let it vanish
Within the waves of your healing soul

Let it flow.

You are not defined by the perspectives
and reflections of others.

No! Your worth is not determined by how
far anyone is willing to go for you.
No! It's not wrong to want to be
loved, respected, and seen.

No! It's not wrong to walk away.
To say no to anything that doesn't serve you.
You are not too much.
You are not too loud.
You are not difficult.

You are beautiful as you are.

Love comes in different ways.
Love is rooted in your soul.
Reflected on the person standing before you,
Every morning, right in your mirror.
Love is you.
And if you can't see it,
It's not because it's not there.

If you listen closely to the call of your heart,
You'll hear the voice that leads you.

It's not about finding yourself.
It's about creating who you want to be.
It's not about finding love somewhere.
It's about seeing love within you.

Note to Self

Next to you, I stand
Looking for the light
For the direction and strength.

Next to you, I hear
I'm within you
The light you seek
It's you!

About the Author

Maria started writing her first poetry book during her journey as a single mom, *From My Healing Heart*. She enjoys life with her children and baby grandson in their home, located in the south suburbs of Chicago.

Printed in the USA
CPSIA information can be obtained
at www.ICGtesting.com
CBHW060001061124
16956CB00035B/396